The Ultimate Leadership Guidebook

All you need to know to become a great leader

AMARPREET SINGH

Publisher - The Thought Flame

THE THOUGHT FLAME
TURNING SPARK INTO FLAME

info@thethoughtflame.com

www.thethoughtflame.com

Table of Contents

Introduction

Believe it or not there are few things in this life that are just as important as leadership. There are many different reasons as to why leadership is important and how effectively leadership can help us to achieve our own personal goals by helping the different people around us first. Whether that reason to is help an entire nation struggling against a catastrophe, making your own business grow in size and productivity or even by helping you to graduate college, leadership is one skill that is absolutely needed in our day-to-day lives.

When there is no leadership present in our lives, everything we do and feel is affected whether we realize it or not. For example children need to have some type of leadership in their lives or how else do they learn to be self-sufficient adults in the future? A business with no leadership cannot grow in size and productivity and in a few years can easily be forced to close its doors. A nation such as the United States could not have grown in size without the form of some type of leader leading it.

Whether we like it or not we all need some form of leader whether it is in our personal lives or in our professional lives as they help us to do the various things that we need to do on a daily basis. Leaders help us to do a variety of things such as find solutions to problems that we would have not normally found by ourselves and to motivate us to do the many things that we may not want to do on a daily basis. That leader can be your supervisor or the owner of the company or you can even be the leader in your own home.

In some form or another we all recognize the need for leadership in our everyday lives in the form of our own political leaders, supervisors in the workplace or parents in the household. We each recognize the need to develop essential leadership skills in every aspect of our lives as this help to keep things running as smoothly as a well-oiled machine.

Leadership is something that is just a normal part of life and that is important to have in every aspect of it. In this eBook I will teach you everything that you need to know about leadership, how to develop the skills both in your personal life and your professional life, what the importance of leadership is and how you can achieve your own goals by helping the people around you

Chapter One: The Importance of Being a Leader and What You Need In Order To Be A Great Leader

One of the most important questions that I am asked on a nearly everyday basis is what does the word leadership even mean? To put it simply leadership is a process in which a specific person is chosen to influence the people around them by influencing the way people feel, the way they act and the way they even think. The perfect kind of leader is one that can help lead people in a certain direction that all will benefit from it and one who can inspire the people around them to become the best that they can be. Without a leader in our lives, our entire world would quickly disintegrate and fall into chaos. Why is this? It is simply because every person on the planet views the world differently than others and as such they will think, behave and act differently than many people around them. A leader can help bring together these differences and have every person who follows them to work towards one common goal.

Leadership in general helps to unite every person together regardless of ethnic background, skin color and religion. Becoming a great leader is not something that happens overnight. Even those in history that we know are great leaders once had trouble securing a loyal following. An example of one such leader is Winston Churchill. When he first arrived on the scene in the early 1930's he tried to warn his people that Hitler was an imminent threat and one that should be taken seriously. Of course as luck would have it, many people didn't see it that way. Many thought that Hitler was a man that they could reason with in a non-aggressive manner and many did not want to start an unnecessary war with Germany. Of course they were all wrong, but still because of his proclamations many people shunned Winston Churchill for him trying to get those to believe that war would be inevitable as long as Hitler led Germany.

As luck would have it many people rejected Churchill's claims and often rejected him as a leader. Everything all changed the moment Germany overstepped their boundaries and began invading other countries. It was only then that people began following Churchill and sought his wisdom on what should be done. Eventually Churchill became Prime Minister of the United Kingdom and led the country into World War II. It was then that nearly every person residing in the United Kingdom followed him with willing faith and loyalty.

While Churchill is an example of a great leader, there are times in our own lives where we will need to be cautious of what I like to call false leaders. These kinds of leaders like to pretend that they are bringing people together toward a common goal when they really aren't. The truth of the matter is not every person is destined to become a great leader. There are some of us who just don't have the necessary skills and attributes that makes a great leader. These people often try to lead the people around them, claiming they are able to inspire thousands while that is simply not the case. These people are often pretending they can do these things when in all reality they can't.

Leadership is something that can either cause greatness in many people or something that can cause great evil in many people. A prime example of this is Hitler himself who, let's face it was a great leader. He somehow managed to inspire people to participate in the deadliest mass genocide and not once did his own people speak against this act. Hitler was able to inspire these people to conduct such heinous acts and they all followed him without question. Another example of a great leader that uses his power for the main purposes of hurting those around him is a leader in the business world. These kinds of leaders are known for abusing their power and using it to exploit the people around them. For example, in a non-profit organization many leaders have been known to use their power to benefit themselves rather than the people they are supposed to be helping.

It is important to know that abusing the power of leadership can cause harm to the people who you want to help because it will help you to become the best leader you can be regardless if you are at home or at work. You need to understand that leadership is power and in order to be used the right way, you need to make sure that you lead people in the right and positive direction.

What Is The Importance of Leadership?

There are a number of reasons as to why leadership is important regardless of where the skill is being utilized. Some of these reasons include:

1. Provides Direction-this can be extremely important especially for those who do not know or understand which direction they are supposed to be working towards. This is incredibly important during times that are unstable in both our personal and professional lives and there will be times when people are going to look to you for some kind of guidance on what they should do.

2. Provide Stability and a Safe Environment-as adults at home and as supervisors in the workplace we are often looked up to in order to provide some stability in the place and to provide a safe environment for both children and co-workers. You will need to be the person who is responsible for teaching your children how to become well-rounded and self-sufficient adults when they become older and you will be the person that your co-workers will look to when they need to be reassured and motivated in the work place.

3. To Provide Guidance On How To Follow Their Passions-both children and adults are no exception to this rule. In order to become self-sufficient and happy adults, people will need to follow their passion in order to wake up everyday feeling successful. You will play a key role in making this dream a reality and can even help in motivating those around you to follow their passions.

4. Provide a Sense of Balance-in today's world it is rather difficult to create the perfect balance between our personal lives and our professional lives. As a leader you can help the people around you to find that perfect balance (even if you don't have it yourself) and help them from becoming overwhelmed on a daily basis.

Today there is a greater need for people to recognize their true potential and to recognize whether or not they have the necessary skills to become a leader and to achieve greatness in their everyday lives. As I have stated multiple times, some people are not destined to become great leaders, but that does not mean they cannot rise above those around them and strive to become a leader in the future. Anything is possible with the right attitude and motivational drive in order to make the dream a reality. Ordinary people like you and I are the ones who have the power to inspire change, to motivate the people around us regardless of the circumstance and can help solve problems that other people usually cannot solve. We can lead others on a path that we want them to follow as long as we have the right mindset to do so and we can help these people work towards a better future in the long run.

The Seven Essential Principles of Leadership

In order to have the right leadership skills that will help us to lead people in the right direction, there are key principles that we must follow in order to achieve this goal. Leadership is not something that just can be done the moment we want it to. It is something that while may come naturally for some people, it will take a lot of practice and patience for ordinary people like you and I. In order to succeed you need to follow these key principles to the T and persevere even when you feel like giving up.

1. You Must Be Patient, Always-have you ever heard of a great leader who always lost his or her patience at the moment of intense pressure? I know that I haven't and it is something that you should never do if you are a leader in both your personal and your professional life. When you are a leader you need to remember that you are in this position for a reason and you have countless people looking to you to lead them in a certain direction. This means laying down a firm hand when it is necessary, not forgetting to lead with love and holding the people around you accountable for their actions. As a leader you need to strive to protect the dignity of the people around you, not to boost the kind of performance you want. This entails you to be patient even at the most trying of times.

If you are the supervisor at your job, your primary goal as a leader will be to train your employees to the best of your ability and to motivate them to complete their daily work tasks. If you are the leader within your household then it will fall onto you to ensure that you raise your children in a loving and patient manner to ensure that they grow up to be self-sufficient and well rounded adults. The key thing to remember here is that you must always be patient regardless of the kind of situation you find yourself in. An impatient leader can inevitably cause disastrous followings in both their professional and personal lives.

2. Be Trusting Of The People Around You and Gain Their Trust In Return-in order for people to follow your lead willing, you need to not only trust them, but they must trust you as well. There are a variety of ways that you can accomplish this such as always sticking to your word, doing the things that your promise to do and never lying to the people that are following your lead.

The best way to gain the trust of the people who are looking to you for leadership is to listen intently on every person that you communicate with. Do not interrupt them or make any kind of comment until they are finished speaking to you. You should also allow these people to make their own decisions whenever you give them the opportunity to do so. You want to do this because it will give them their own sense of worth and you will be able to teach them how to become a leader in their own right.

Remember, you need to trust the people around you as well. The best advice that I can give you is to listen to the people around you and to listen to their suggestions before making your own. Also never assume what a person is going to do or how they are going to act because you may be surprised when they do something you least expect.

3. Be As Kind As Possible to The People Around You-one of the greatest attributes of any leader is how they treat the people who look to them for leadership with both patience and kindness. It is extremely important to show the people that you are leading both enthusiasm and encouragement so that they can accomplish all of the things they and you want them to such as paperwork or even cleaning up after themselves.

The best way that I can describe this is to imagine that you the person you are dealing with is a bank account. Now every now and then you will want to "deposit" a certain amount into what I like to call their emotional accounts so that before you know it the account can grow until it is nearly overflowing. The way that this works in real practices is that you want to strive to compliment and praise the people around you at least three times a week or better daily. Using this technique will help to show that you are showing the right amount of kindness to the people around you and that you are causing a heavy flow of enthusiasm that these people will be more than willing to follow you in the long run.

4. Always Be Honest and Truthful-the key to becoming a great leader in the future is to remain as honest and truthful as possible regardless of where you are, either at home or at work. In these places you will most likely be leading with a style that I like to call "leading with love." The way that you lead with love is to encourage the people following you and to give them kind and loving feedback as often as possible as this will not only help yourself to grow, but it will help your company or household to grow as well.

Let's be honest, leading with love is something that most people have not heard of before and it something that may seem foreign to them. It can be so strange in fact that it can cause people to come out of their comfort zone. However, although it may be uncomfortable for many people, it is one of the best and healthiest ways to lead people as this will earn you great respect and trust in the long run.

5. Do Not Be Selfish-when you are a leader in your personal life or in your professional life there really is no time to be selfish. You need to remember that people are looking to you to lead them towards a certain direction and if you suddenly become selfish and only care about yourself, your family or corporation will go towards the direction that you want them to go. When you are a leader, it is your primary mission to worry about the many people around you than you worry for yourself as they are the most important.

One of the primary duties that you will have as a leader is the act of delegating to others. While this is far from fun it will teach you to become selfless in time. This will give you the opportunity to show the people around you how much you respect them, which can help increase your own following in the long run.

6. You Need To Be Able To Forgive People-while I am no exception to this, nearly every person out there today has a problem forgiving people who have wronged them. As a leader you cannot and do not have the ability to hold on to grudges nor can you walk around treating people like dirt if they wronged you in some way. Forgiving people is never easy. On the contrary it is a very agonizing process and one that hardly leads to any kind of happy ending, but it is one that will earn you a large amount of respect from your followers. Before you get upset you need to understand that I am not telling you to ignore any kind of company policies or rules that you have in place for disagreeing with someone. What I am telling you is to attempt to soften your heart even just a little bit and be open minded to forgiving others regardless of what they have done to you.

Forgiving people is not the easiest thing in the world to do. I know that better than anybody. While it may not be the easiest it is certainly one of the most rewarding things that you can do in your life and is one thing that you should do if you plan on becoming a great leader.

7. Be Dedicated In Whatever It Is You Do- whether you are leading a political party or whether you are leading your family at a family reunion, regardless of what you are doing make sure that you are dedicated to the task at hand. As a dedicated leader it is important that you stick to whatever values you may have and make sure that you do not stray too far from them. You need to remain dedicated to whatever task you have set to follow, regardless of what the other people around you may think. Remember the only thing that matters is if the task you are setting out to do is important to you.

Chapter Two: How Motivation Can Help You To Become A Great Leader

Is there really a need for motivation when it comes to leadership? The answer to this question is an absolute yes. So, what is motivation? Why is it important in leadership? Motivation itself is the process that is used that can influence a person to work towards their long term goals whether they are professional or personal. The thing that you need to know about motivation is that it is not something that you can see with the naked eye. It is something that is more of a mental act and is something that you can feel rather than see. Motivation can be used to describe how a person feel towards a certain task and is the driving force behind getting that person to finish the task they are set to do.

There have been several cases recorded when researchers have tried to study how motivation acts on the mind of a human and what it actually does to a person, but of course none of these studies have been successful. Researches have tried to come up with several theories on how motivation acts upon the human mind such as drive reduction theories and Maslow's Hierarchy pyramid. These theories are as close to narrowing down exactly how motivation works as we will ever get.

What Are Drive Reduction Theories?

If you don't know what a drive reduction theory is, don't worry. You wouldn't be the only one. Drive reduction theories are theories that are used to explain how people use motivation in order to reduce the needs of their body and to maintain a healthy physiological state. The best way that I could explain this is to think of the simple task of eating. Why do we do it? We do it simply because we have to and we do it every morning in order to decrease the amount of times that we have to eat during the day. This simple task can also be referred to as seeking a state of Homeostasis. Homeostasis is the term used to explain the main drive to a drive theory and it is the act of maintain the human body until it reaches the perfect equilibrium.

While drive theories are great at explaining and helping us to understand what motivation can do for people, it does fail in helping us to understand what are the several important factors needed for motivation to occur. Some of the factors needed for motivation are:

1. Not Being Motivated by Internal Needs-what this implies is that a person will have no problem doing something if it means supporting a certain cause regardless if it causes some kind of harm to their actual body. For example, you may have seen thousands of people go on a hunger strike to save a historic building from being demolished or to obtain their own right, regardless of the fact that they are depriving their body of much need food. To these kinds of people, their beliefs and causes are more important than their bodies.

2. Will Remain Motivated Even After Their Internal Needs Have Been Satisfied-what this factor implies is that a person will continue to feel motivated, even if they have done everything that they have to in order to meet their internal needs. For example, let's say that a person has just eaten a large lunch. Well after an hour later the suddenly eat again. It is not because they are hungry, but rather because they are bored or they just want a particular item. They will continue eating without feeling hungry.

3. People will be motivated by using incentives both internally and externally-what this means is that a person will find a way to keep themselves motivated both by fulfilling a new of theirs both for their body and for their desire. So for example, let's take a woman who is on a strict diet. She will do whatever it takes to make sure that she loses the weight that she needs to lose. If she heads out to eat with a group of friends she is more likely to choose to eat a salad rather than eat anything unhealthy because of this factor. Now, this doesn't only apply to dieting, it can also apply to virtually anything from quitting smoking cigarettes or even their own career.

The Difference Between Extrinsic Motivation and Intrinsic Motivation

There are different forms of motivation and they primarily come in either intrinsic motivation or extrinsic motivation or even a combination of the two. There are many differences between these two types of motivation and it is important that you know what that difference is. Intrinsic motivation is when a person uses the art of motivation to benefit only themselves. For example let's say we have a writer. What is the primary reason that they write? Not because they have to do it. They write just for the sake of the enjoyment of it.

Now let's take at what extrinsic motivation is. Extrinsic motivation is a form of motivation that is primarily used to help the person earn a great reward in the end. So for example let's take your average author who works their butts off on a daily basis trying to come up with the most amazing story they could ever write. The end reward they would love to earn is either to get published or to become rich and famous off of their writing.

Regardless if a person is using either extrinsic or intrinsic motivation to help them achieve their goals, each kind of motivation needs their own form of incentives in order to prove effective. What exactly is an incentive? It is a type of stimulus that can come from the environment that helps a person reach the goals they have set for themselves. A prime example of a stimulus would be for a student to get an A on an exam of a term paper so that they are able to pass their class for the semester.

What is Maslow's Hierarchy

Around 1970 there was a famous psychologist that went by the name Abraham Maslow. Maslow came up with a theory regarding motivation and he claimed that a hierarchy of different needs were what motivated people. To come up with this theory Maslow study a variety of people and took note of what it was that motivated them. This theory is one that many psychologists still use today. Maslow Hierarchy goes as follows:

1. Level One: Physiological-in the first level of this hierarchy this is where the basic psychological needs of people are used as motivational tools. These basic needs can consist of security, water and food. These basic needs are what every human on the planet needs on a daily basis just to survive. The one basic need that is the most critical than the rest is the natural feeling of being safe and it is one of the factors that humans utilize the most to survive. If you are doubtful just think of children. Young children look to their parents for safety and comfort and as they grow older this feeling never goes away.

2. Level Two: The Need to Feel As If You Belong and Loved-the second level of this hierarchy consist of the basic need to feel as if a person feels loved and if they feel like they belong. While this may like a strange motivational factor, this is another factor that many people use to this very day in order to motivate themselves. This need is again used primarily by small children and sometimes this even overrides their natural instinct to feel safe. Children who do not have this basic need met are often hospitalized due to neglect and tend to suffer in their relationships in the future.

3. Level Three: Basic Self-Esteem-the third level within this hierarchy is one motivational factor that many people use primarily in their professional lives and that is the need to build their self-esteem and to earn some self-respect. The need to be accepted by the people around you is one of our basic human needs and it is one that you should never be ashamed of admitting that you have and this need will carry from your personal life to your professional life.

When this basic need is not met, people tend to become imbalanced in every aspect of their lives. In severe cases some people in fact tend to develop an inferiority complex to the point they constantly suffer from low self-esteem which can lead to them having damaging relationships with the people around them.

4. Level Four: The Need To Understand One's Full Potential-this level of the hierarchy consists of the need to understand a person's own self potential as a factor leading to their motivation.

This growing needs is what enables people to work to the best of their ability and what allows them to grow as an individual. There are many people who have this desire whether it is a first time mother who wants to be the best mother that she can be or a college basketball player that wants to make it to the big leagues. This factor is one that every person craves in every aspect of their life and is what can help to drive their own motivation.

While the needs of a few individuals is what drives their motivation, there ar some instances when people find a lack of motivation. This can be due to many reason but the most common is because of factors that are popular in both our society and our culture. Regardless of that fact there are a variety of factors that can help motivate us on a daily basis such as the need to eat, drink socialize, feel as if we belong and the need to feel loved. These needs are what can help a person to achieve their long-term goals or simply to get through the day. Whatever these needs are they are determined by how a person perceives life in general and what kind of importance they want their life to hold.

Is Motivation Important?

While many people not realize it, motivation itself is extremely important. It is something that is needed in order for us to do the many things that we want to accomplish in our short lives such as fame or financial freedom. Motivation is the primary thing in our lives that drives us to do all the things we need and want to do on a daily basis. Can you even imagine how difficult life would be without motivation driving us forward?

There is no law stating that only positive emotions are what can spur on motivation. Motivation can be a product of negative emotions as well such as a motive behind a man killing

33

another man. Another example of a negative emotion that can help to motivate us is stress. We have all been stressed out at one point or another in our lives and it has helped us to overcome great obstacles that have come across our paths. However, there is a downside to stress and that is that people tend to become very narrow minded and can even become paralyzed from stress to the point they do not want to do anything.

So the question remains, is motivation something that is more important in our professional lives or more important in our personal lives? The answer to this is that motivation is important in both areas of our lives and it is important to find that key balance as to what motivates us and what stresses us out. Why is this? Well, to start while we spend many more hours at work then we do at home motivation is going to play a critical role in our professional lives. However, it is important to stay motivated at home simply because this is the place we feel the most comfortable and that being said this is the place that we tend to let our guard down the most.

For many years now there has been a debate raging on what kind of role motivation plays in a person's professional life and whether or not if a person meets their goals if that is what causes motivation to occur in the first place. In my opinion this is not the case. People work hard so that they can reach whatever goals they have set for themselves. The driving force behind a person's motivation is what leads them to accomplish these goals, not the other way around. In my opinion anytime a company wishes to motivate its staff should consider offering some kind of incentive or bonus as a way to motivate them. This bonus or incentive can be as simple as money and you would be surprised what lengths people are willing to go to in order to make a little extra money on the side.

How Does Motivation Affect Human Behavior?

Of course with every person motivation itself will vary in different degrees ranging from intense motivation to little or almost nothing. This is why if you were to stand back and study a group of people from afar you would notice how each person is motivated differently and what are the causes behind that motivation.One of the ways that researchers have studied what kind of affect motivation has on human behavior is to use what is known as a behavior matrix. A behavior matrix is a tool used to separate people into four different groups solely based on different motivational factors. These four groups are: Producers, Relators, Motivators and Processors. In this section we will go through what each section of these groups are and how to recognize what kind of people fit into these categories.

1. Group One: Motivators-the kind of people that fit into this section of the behavior matrix are the type of people who have a knack for motivating whoever is around them. These people are very outspoken, excited and enthusiastic about whatever kind of situation they are in and are the type of people that are extremely fun to be around. The main factor that drives the motivation for these people is the need to feel unique and this is what causes them to have a real talent for motivating themselves and the people around them.

2. Group Two: Producers-the kind of people that fit into this group of the behavior matrix are the type of people who are very goal oriented. The people that fit into this group can be described as being very confident in themselves, very down to earth and are very strong minded about the direction their lives take. These kind of people can be described as getting straight to the point without cutting corners and are very adept at working as hard as they need to in order to reach the goals they have set for themselves.

3. Group Three: Processors-the kind of people that are in this group of the behavior matrix are the kind of people that think whatever it they are going to do very thoroughly before acting upon their actions. These kind of people are very logical about the things they do and have a very serious mindset. These types of people tend to be very organized in every aspect of their lives and they have a knack for understand the environment they find themselves in making it easy for them to drive the motivation they need in order to get things done.

4. Group Four: Relators-the kind of people that fit into this category of the behavior matrix are the most loyal and supportive people you will ever come across. These people can be described as be the most trustworthy, friendly and caring people you will ever come across and many people often seek them out if they are ever needed. Relators are the kind of people who are great at creating lasting relationship with the people around them and can easily get along with any person they meet in their lives. Because these people have the need to feel wanted and loved by the people in their lives, the main factor that drives their motivation is mainly because of this cause.

What is the reason that it is important to know how each person fits into the different categories within the behavior matrix? It is important because if you happen to be the owner of a business it is great to understand exactly what you can do to motivate your employees. If you work for a company you can easily figure out what it is that motivates you so that you can use it to your advantage to help motivate yourself while you are at work. While money is a easy way to motivate people both in their professional or their personal lives, there are better and more efficient ways to motivate people just by knowing what kind of person they are and what it is that can otherwise motivate them.

Chapter Three: The Importance of Both Motivation And Leadership In One's Professional Life

So far in this eBook you have learned how motivation and leadership help to play a critical role in the lives of many people and how it helps these people to be more productive regardless if they are at home or at work. You now know that motivation is not just something that can be used to help a person reach their goals, but it is something that can also be used to help maintain a person's behavior in any kind of situation they may find themselves in and can help get the person anything he or she may want out of life such as financial freedom or to even graduate college.

Remember, leadership is just as important as motivation because as a leader in your home or in your career it is your responsibility to ensure that your employees or your family are just as motivated as you are.So, when you are combining both leadership and motivation, how can you use these two in a workplace environment? In this chapter you will learn how you can use them effectively and use them to bring out the best in your employees and yourself.

How To Add Motivation In Your Workplace

Remember, motivation is a stimulus that you will need to use in your workplace as a means to help energize your employees and yourself and to elicit the kind of behavior you are looking for. As long as you use motivation properly you can get whatever it is you want such as an increase in the amount of sales you make or an increase of the amount of work that is generated on a daily basis. In my opinion motivation is one of the most important factors that can be within any workplace just for the simple reason that the way an employee performs at work represents the nature of the very company itself.

Explaining how effective motivation can be in the workplace may be more tricky than it seems. We know that by increasing the amount of motivation that you generate can heavily impact the amount of productivity that an employee generates, it is harder to actually pinpoint how much motivation an employer can use and how to use just enough of it that it does not lose its effectiveness. One thing is for certain: many companies nowadays recognize how important motivation is in the workplace and now many companies do whatever they need to do to ensure their employees stay motivated throughout their time working for that company. Understanding how to manage motivation can help employers understand how much motivation they should strive to help their employees get and to understand when they may be asking for too much motivation.

In the workplace it is not uncommon to hear of salary being on the most commonly used motivational tools out there. It is the reason why many people today continue to work at places they hate being employees at, simply because they are willing to be unhappy because the pay is the only thing that is good about the place. While the pay rate may be great, money alone does not guarantee that an employee will work to the best of their ability and is not enough to motivate them to increase their own productivity.

That is why it is important to know that even employees who are paid better than most in a company, but who do not feel motivated at work are more likely to slack off and miss deadlines than those who are kept motivated on a daily basis. As an employer you will need to know what it is that motivates your employees and how you can use those motivational factors to bring out the best in your team and help to ensure each employee produces the highest quality work as possible.

The Internal and External Factors of Motivation

When you have employees that are highly motivated on a daily basis, there are many ways that a company can benefit from it. These benefits can include:

1. Employees are most likely to improve the overall quality of their work by find new and creative ways to do so.

2. Employees are more likely to pay close attention to the detail of their work and are more likely to produce the highest quality work as they possibly can.

3. Employees are more likely to be more productive than employees who are not motivated. These employees are also more likely to meet their deadlines in an efficient and timely manner.

The point of the matter is that you should always strive to motivate your employees. Motivation is just something that you cannot go wrong with. There are many advantages to motivating your employees such as increasing the amount of innovation within your company, help your employees to produce the highest quality of work they are capable of producing and increasing the amount of productivity within your company as a whole. While these benefits may seem a bit vague, the main thing you need to take away from this is that motivation will not harm your company whatsoever. Motivating your employees is something that is completely free to do and does not take a lot of effort on your part. As long as you have the right managers in place that can in fact lead your employees into motivation, you will have no problem reaping the reward of having motivated employees working for you.

Different Motivational Theories

From the perspective of a manager or a business owner, there are other ways to ensure their employees stay motivation without having to use motivation itself. In order to know what you can use as a motivational tool to help motivate your employees to the point of raising productivity, you first need to understand and grasp the basic concept of what it is that motivates each individual employee. As a manager or business owner you can easily do this by simply using positive techniques and incentives rather than using negativity and negative incentives.

The kind of motivational factors you will use will solely be based upon what is known as organizational behavior. This is a form of basic psychology and the way that it works in terms of motivation is that if motivation is used correctly employees are able to focus on the task at hand and achieve more in the long run while in their professional setting. These employees will more likely work tirelessly to achieve their long term goal regardless of what it will cost them in terms of mental and physical exhaustion.

In order to make this concept simple to understand I will explain a variety of different theories out there today that are used to help employers find the most effect motivational factors to use in a professional setting. There are four different theories and they are known as need-based theories, cognitive process theories, behavioral theories and job-based theories. In this section I will go through each theory individually so you can get a chance to understand how each theory can play a crucial role in motivating the employees that may work for you.

1. Need-Based Theory-when you are talking about motivation, it is clear that it can be define just by the way people fill their basic human needs. Of course with every different kind of person these needs will vary greatly from basic human desires such as finding love for finding some way to belong to a certain group to fulfilling basic needs such as eating and drinking to sustain one's life. The best example of this is Maslow's Hierarchy which I outlined in the previous chapter.

In Maslow's Hierarchy Maslow came up with the theory that a person is motivated by separate basic needs such as raising their own self-esteem, sustaining one's life by simply eating and drinking and filling the need to belong. As correct and straightforward as this theory sounds, many employees do not know of it and therefore do not help to fill these needs of their employees and don't understand how to motivate their employees in this way.

2. Behavioral Theory-the whole point of this kind of motivational theory is that an employer can motivate their employee simply by conditioning them. What does this mean? It means that an employer can use the tactic of a reward system in order to motivate their employees and can help to stimulate the amount of positive and negative energy that is lingering within the workplace.

The only way that I can explain this theory so that it is easy to understand is to take a sales job as an example. In a sales job the money an employee makes depends solely on the amount of sales they achieve in a weekly basis. Because of this an employees earning potential is virtually limitless so an employee is more likely concerned with making as many sales as possible then anything else. As an employer you can help your employee to increase the amount of sales they make simply by rewarding them further with every sale they make.

3. Job-Based Theory-in a professional setting employees are responsible for completing any task they are given for that particular work day. Because of this many employees will feel obligated to ensure that their tasks are completed simply because that is their job and it is their duty to contribute as much as they can to the company they work for. Other than duty a person may have a variety of incentives given to them based upon them completing their job successfully such as health insurance or 401K incentives. These benefits may play a role in how motivated a person is at their job and may even keep them interested in whatever job they are doing. It is also known that employees who feel more connected to their job and want to be their are more often to feel motivated than others who simply do not want to be there.

4. Cognitive Process Theory-this kind of theory is geared towards what kind of expectation the employee holds in regards to the company they work for and what they expect to earn in return for the amount of work they do on a weekly basis. This can help both employees and employers alike to understand the reward for motivating the people around them and are more likely to spend more time focusing on how to motivate the people they work with.

How Can You Motivate The People Around You?

There are so many ways that you can motivate the people around you as their leader that if I explained each of those ways this book would be more than 100 pages long. However, I will give you a small list on the easiest ways that you can motivate people and increase the productivity of those around you.

1. Try To Give Your Employees The Chance To Work Alongside The Things That Interest Them-it is no secret that those who do work that they do not like doing are more likely never to complete their work or to meet their strict deadlines. However, if you give an employee a project that you know falls within their interests, they are more likely to complete it well before their deadline and with more enthusiasm than they originally elicit.

2. Try To Take Your Employees Future Into Account-one of the most important things that you can do as a leader in your company is to care about what kind of future your employees will have while they are under your wing. You may be surprised the direction that your employees want to follow and the way that you can help them is to mentor and guide them to help them reach the goal they want.

3. Be Interested In The Balance of Your Employees Personal and Professional Life-we are all human. We all have jobs and we all have families that both demand our attention. Your employee is no different. As a leader you can try to be more understanding of this delicate balancing act to the best of your ability. If you can try to make flexible schedules for your employees and take into consideration if one of your employees has an important doctors appointment that he or she cannot miss. This little bit of consideration can go a long way in earning respect from those you work with.

There are many ways and reasons that you should try to motivate the people that work with you. Not only will it earn you a tremendous amount of respect from the people around you, but it will also help you to increase the amount of work and productivity that is made on a daily basis. Regardless of how you do it or why you do it, as a leader you should always strive to motivate the people around you to help bring out the best in all of you.

Conclusion

In order to become a great leader in the long run, there are a variety of different things that you must do in order to have people follow of you. We discussed how honesty can play a critical role in how people view and respect you, you need to lead with kindness and love to increase that respect and you need to motivate the people around you so that all of you can work towards that common goal.

Motivation is just as important as leading the people that look to you for guidance. Without motivation our lives would be pretty dull. Without this, do not expect to become a great leader in the long run. Motivation is something that is needed on a daily basis especially if you wish to have a life that is running as smoothly as possible.

You need to keep in mind that not every person on the planet is destined to be a leader. Some of us do not have the necessary skills that is needed to be a leader. You need to understand that in order to become a great leader, a bit of science and steps need to be followed to allow for greatness. In order to become a great leader you need to use all of the tools and methods I have outlined correctly so that you can impact the people who follow you in the right way with motivation.

Hopefully by reading this Leadership eBook you have learned everything there is to know about becoming a great leader, what are the necessary steps you need to take in order to reach the status of a great leader and how motivation itself can help you to become a great leader in the long run.

About Us:

The Thought Flame is committed to add value to its customers through various books, online courses and other resources. You can learn more about us and our books at www.thethoughtflame.com.

Don't forget to check out our amazing **online video courses** at www.thethoughtflame.com/courses/ to take your knowledge to another level.

To check out our **extraordinary collection of diet/cookbooks**, visit

http://www.thethoughtflame.com/category/non-fictional/cookbooks/ .

As a part of our valued relationship with our customers, we keep providing you free promotional books, courses and other stuff on subscribing with us on our site. We have a strict anti-spam policy and assure you no spam mails will be sent to your mailbox.

To subscribe with us, visit

www.thethoughtflame.com.

Like our work and would like to say thanks?

Buy us a cup of coffee at

www.thethoughtflame.com/coffee/

Author:

Amarpreet Singh is an avid learner and his passion for education has made him travel, work and study all across the world. He holds three masters degrees, including MBA, from top universities in Asia.

He is author of dozens of books, many of which are Amazon's bestseller, varying in various topics and categories. He also teaches many online courses having thousands of students across the world.

He has a keen interest in international affairs, economics, global poverty and politics, financial markets and entrepreneurship, and strives to be part of a community that shares the same passion.

He has worked as consultant with organizations like Airbus and The World Bank.

He loves travelling and learning about new cultures, and has been fortunate to live/work/travel/study in countries like India, China, Korea, US, South Africa, Japan, Philippines, Singapore, Canada etc., and learn about the culture and lifestyle in each of them.

To check out more of his work, visit

www.thethoughtflame.com